Official Mensa
Puzzle Book

You'd Better Be Really Smart

BRAIN BAFFLERS

Tim Sole
Rod Marshall

Sterling Publishing Co., Inc.
New York

Library of Congress Cataloging-in-Publication Data Available

10 9 8 7 6 5 4 3 2 1

Published by Sterling Publishing Co., Inc.
387 Park Avenue South, New York, NY 10016
© 2003 by Tim Sole and Rod Marshall
Distributed in Canada by Sterling Publishing
℅ Canadian Manda Group, One Atlantic Avenue, Suite 105
Toronto, Ontario, Canada M6K 3E7
Distributed in Great Britain by Chrysalis Books
64 Brewery Road, London N7 9NT, England
Distributed in Australia by Capricorn Link (Australia) Pty. Ltd.
P.O. Box 704, Windsor, NSW 2756, Australia

Sterling ISBN 1-4027-0543-3

CONTENTS

Acknowledgments

Our thanks are due to many people, without whose help this book would not have been possible. To name but some:

The London Staple Inn Actuarial Society, which publishes *The Actuary* and which published its predecessor, *Fiasco*. Many of the puzzles in this book have been published in one of these magazines.

To the editors of *The Actuary* and *Fiasco* for their support and encouragement to us as puzzle editors.

To those listed below (and we apologize if we have overlooked anyone) for creating, assisting with or suggesting puzzles that we have used: 9–David Sole, 22–Maurice Steinhart, 36–Edward Johnston, 56–Chris Munro, 59–Roger Gilbert, 65–Chris Cole, 71–Maurice Steinhart, 74–Charles G. Groeschell, 81–Alan Wood, 89–Hugh Norman, 90–David Sole, 91–Alan Wilson, John Gemmell, Tom Grimes, 92–Terry Wills, Francis Heaney, 93–D.P. Laurie, 94–Dennis Lister, 100–Tim Lund, 126–Frank Guaschi.

—Tim Sole and Rod Marshall

PUZZLES

1. A, B, C, and D each represent a different word or phrase, and they have a common theme. What are the four words or phrases and what is the theme?

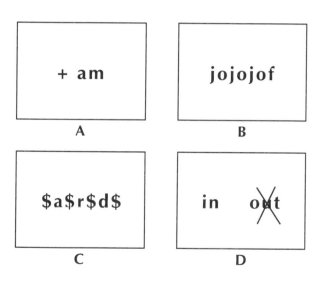

Answer, page 75

2. In the following list of commonly known words, you are given the central letters. Each word begins and ends with the same two letters in the same order. How many words can you complete?

1. ****ca****   2. ****bl****   3. ****eepi****   4. ****adac****

5. ****ur****   6. ****gib****   7. ****risco****   8. ****epsa****

Answer, page 74

3.

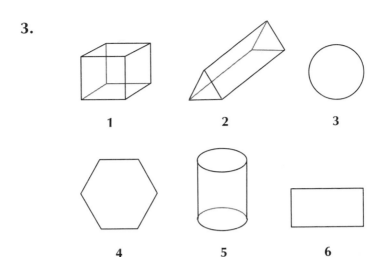

1   2   3

4   5   6

Thinking laterally, which of the following are the seventh and eighth shapes in the series above?

4. Find a ten-digit number that:
   • can be described as having m digits between the m's, n digits between the n's, and so on, and
   • whose first digit is a prime number, the two-digit number formed by its second and third digits is a prime number, the three-digit number formed by its fourth, fifth, and sixth digits is three times a prime number, and the four-digit number formed by its last four digits is also a prime number.

Answer, page 76

5. How can a horseshoe be cut into six pieces with two straight cuts? There are three different ways.

Answer, page 66

6. A, B, C, and D each represent a different word or phrase, and they have a common theme. What are the four words or phrases and what is the theme?

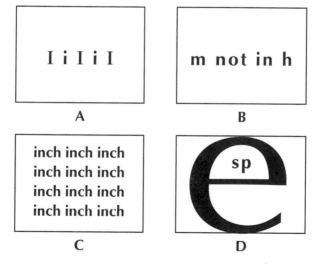

I i I i I

A

m not in h

B

inch inch inch
inch inch inch
inch inch inch
inch inch inch

C

sp

D

Answer, page 68

7. What two-word phrase could form the first and fourth rows of the diagram so that each column contains a four-letter word?

S	E	O	A	L	O
E	A	T	C	S	E

Answer, page 67

8. In an international soccer tournament, the scores in a certain round were as follows:

Argentina	0	N. Ireland	0
Belgium	1	Wales	4
England	0	Scotland	1
France	1	Spain	2
Germany	1	Brazil	1
Italy	3	Denmark	1
Peru	2	Cameroon	0
Poland	?	Portugal	?

Each score is related to the name of the corresponding country. Crack the code to figure out what the score was in the final match.

Answer, page 84

9. Complete the grid using all the letters below so that each row and column containing two or more squares is a word when read from left to right or from top to bottom.

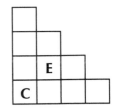

A D E F I N S T

Answer, page 79

10. Each of these crossword clues is a full anagram of the answer:

ACROSS

2. I hire parsons (12)

3. On tip (5)

4. Date's up (4,3)

5. Is a lane (2,5)

6. Here come dots (3,5,4)

7. Eleven + two (6+3)

8. Must anger (9)

DOWN

1. No untidy clothes (3,6,6)

Answer, page 79

11. A, B, C, and D each represent a different word or phrase, and they have a common theme. What are the four words or phrases and what is the theme?

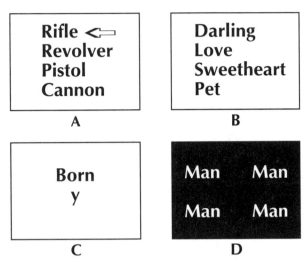

A

B

C

D

Answer, page 74

12. The answer to the first of these is "29 days in February in a leap year." Complete the rest.

29 D in F in a L Y

12 S of the Z

7 W of the A W

54 C in a D (with the J)

32 D F, at which W F

18 H on a G C

4 Q in a G

14 P in a S

Answer, page 67

13. There are five men in five houses. Each man comes from a different town (all genuine names), has a different pet, and supports a different rugby team. From the following clues, determine which man supports the Waratahs and, if different, which man has a kea.

The five houses are in a row and each is a different color.

The man who has the kangaroo lives next to the man from Woy Woy.

Mr. Brown supports the Brumbies.

The man from Wagga Wagga lives in the blue house.

Mr. Green lives in the mauve house.

The man from Bong Bong has a kookaburra.

Mr. White comes from Aka Aka.

Mr. Gray lives on the left in the first house.

The red house is to the right of and adjacent to the yellow house.

The man from Peka Peka supports the Hurricanes.

The man who has a koala lives next door to the man from Wagga Wagga.

Mr. Black has a kiwi.

The man in the middle house supports the Sharks.

The man in the red house supports the Crusaders.

The maroon house is next to Mr. Gray's house.

Answer, page 70

14. Find a four-digit number that is equal to the square of the sum of the number formed by its first two digits and the number formed by its last two digits, and is exactly 1,000 different from another four-digit number with the same property.

Answer, page 69

15. A, B, C, and D each represent a different word or phrase, and they have a common theme. What are the four words or phrases and what is the theme?

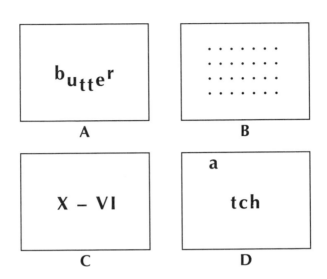

butter

A

B

X – VI

C

a
tch

D

Answer, page 67

16. Two lists of words have been created. Embedded in one list are the 26 letters of the alphabet in their correct order. Embedded in the other list are the 26 letters of the alphabet in reverse order.

The alphabet (forward or backward, as appropriate) has been removed from each list, and the spaces between words have been closed up. In each case the following letters remain:

D O E B O S I T E L E R O E U I U S I G U A T G L I E A E S T

All the words in the original two lists have at least three letters, and each word in each list includes at least one letter from the above string and at least one letter of the alphabet that was subsequently removed. Find two lists of words—one containing the 26 letters of the alphabet in their correct order and the second containing the 26 letters in reverse alphabetical order—that meet these conditions.

Answer, page 68

• 12 •

17. The Golden Bay Dining Tour itinerary includes six dinners. Five holidaymakers following this itinerary are all at different stages of the tour. One holidaymaker has dined once so far, and the other four have dined two, three, four and five times. The dining itinerary begins and ends with dinner at The Old School Cafe, and the four dinners between are at four other restaurants and always in the same order.

From this information and the information below, determine where each holidaymaker comes from, the name of the restaurant at which the holidaymaker last dined, and the name of the restaurant at which the holidaymaker will be dining next.

1. Ann, who is not from Christchurch, will dine next at the Farewell Spit Cafe.

2. Ben does not come from Auckland.

3. Cathy, who last dined at Milliways Restaurant, will not be dining at the Collingwood Tavern next.

4. David is not from Auckland or Dunedin, and dined last at somewhere other than the Collingwood Tavern.

5. Emma comes from Hamilton.

6. The next person to dine at the Wholemeal Cafe did not last dine at the Collingwood Tavern.

7. Ben, the person from Christchurch, the person who last dined at the Farewell Spit Cafe and the person who will next dine at Milliways Restaurant are four of the five holidaymakers.

8. Neither the person from Wellington nor the person from Dunedin will be dining next at the Collingwood Tavern.

Answer, page 91

18. Although this puzzle seems easy when you hear the answer, few people are able to get all four answers right the first time. In fact, three out of four can be considered a very good score. Name the northernmost, southernmost, easternmost, and westernmost states of the U.S.A.

Answer, page 67

19. A calendar comprises a stand and two printed cubes. Each day both cubes are positioned in the stand to read the day's date, which can of course be any number from 01 to 31. How are the numbers arranged on the cubes?

Answer, page 69

20. A, B, C and D each represent a different word or phrase, and they have a common theme. What are the four words or phrases and what is the theme?

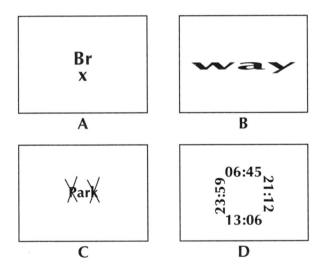

Answer, page 70

21. Tennis is a sport in which you can you take a container that is half full of balls, add another ball, and still have a container that is half full. True or false?

Answer, page 71

22. What is the missing number?

$$9 \quad 22 \quad 24 \quad 12 \quad \underline{\quad} \quad 4 \quad 13$$

Answer, page 73

23. Each of these crossword clues is a full anagram of the answer:

ACROSS

1. Stopped? No (9)

3. The or (5)

4. Moon starer (10)

5. Name for ship (3,8)

6. Tender names (11)

7. Has to pilfer (1,10)

8. They see (3,4)

DOWN

2. No city dust here (3,11)

Answer, page 72

24. A, B, C, and D each represent a different word or phrase, and they have a common theme. What are the four words or phrases and what is the theme?

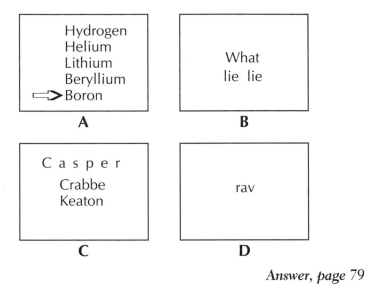

Hydrogen
Helium
Lithium
Beryllium
⟹ Boron

A

What
lie lie

B

C a s p e r
Crabbe
Keaton

C

rav

D

Answer, page 79

25. The first ten natural numbers have been arranged into columns according to a certain rule, as shown below:

1	4	3
2	5	7
6	9	8
10		

A. The numbers 11 and 12 would appear in the same column as each other, but which one?

B. If the arrangement were continued indefinitely, what would be the final entry in the third column?

Answer, page 70

26. Although at first you may not think so, this paragraph is unusual. A quick study will show that it has capitals, commas, and full stops so that punctuation, as far as I know, is satisfactory. But this paragraph is most unusual, and I would hazard my opinion that you do not know why. Should you look at it backwards, or in a mirror, or both, you will find just rubbish, so obviously that is not a way to a solution. Ability at crosswords and similar things may assist you, but I doubt it. If you still do not know what this paragraph is all about, you could go back and start again, but you should not find it particularly difficult. I warn you to watch for your sanity though, as this paragraph is unnatural. Can you work out why? Good luck!

Answer, page 84

27. Security at Prime Palace is a very straightforward affair. There are no keys, just simple bracelets on which are hung five numbers. Access to sensitive areas is then granted by presenting the bracelet in a way that shows a five-digit prime number. Given that a bracelet can be read clockwise or counterclockwise and there are five numbers to start from, the chances of picking a prime number at random can therefore be as low as one in ten.

Sounds simple? Well, as an extra check, you are asked to swap your bracelet for one of the same color at every door, so you need to know for your color the full set of possible prime numbers.

Although the system worked well for many years, it was almost abandoned when the queen remarried. The new king simply could not remember his numbers! He therefore was given a special bracelet that always produced a prime however it was presented, and he was never asked to swap bracelets.

What numbers were on the king's bracelet?

Answer, page 73

28. Prime Palace (see puzzle 27 above) now wants to move to a six-figure system. Will there be a suitable new bracelet for the king?

Answer, page 72

29. Place the numbers from 1 to 19 in the diagram in such a way that the numbers in each of the 15 straight lines of small hexagons have the same total, namely 38. It is not easy, but it can be done!

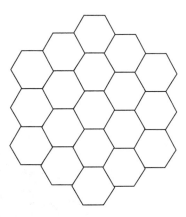

Answer, page 76

30. A, B, C and D each represent a different word or phrase, and they have a common theme. What are the four words or phrases and what is the theme?

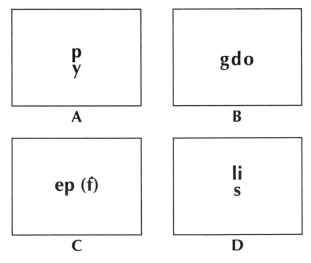

Answer, page 73

31. Readers are no doubt familiar with "word search" puzzles, where various (usually related) words are hidden in an array and the puzzle is simply to find them. The words may run horizontally, vertically, or diagonally, may run in either direction, or may overlap, but they must run in a straight line. Often there are letters in the array that are not used.

Construct a word search puzzle using the words ONE, TWO, THREE, FOUR, FIVE, SIX, SEVEN, EIGHT, NINE, TEN, ELEVEN, and TWELVE in the grid below.

When completed, the diagram below will have just one unused letter.

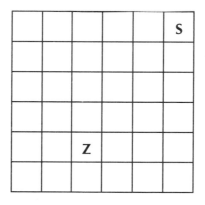

Answer, page 71

32. The name of which country includes both a "q" and a "z"?

Answer, page 73

33. Can it be said that the six words below are in alphabetical order?

almost   belt   dirt   know   jot   most

Answer, page 73

34. Zoe's solitaire board consists of 28 holes set out in a triangle as shown in the diagram. The game starts with a peg in every hole except the central one (shaded in the diagram) and is played in the usual way. Each move consists of jumping a peg over an adjacent peg into a hole, with the peg over which the jump is made then being removed from the board. The aim is to be left with only one peg on the board.

Through trial and error, Zoe has convinced herself that the puzzle is impossible. Can you help her prove this?

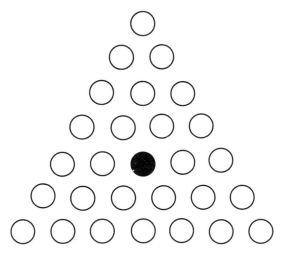

Answer, page 74

35. X and XSUM are two variables related to each other as follows:

XSUM equals the total of the digits comprising X

X equals $(XSUM)^3$

One solution is XSUM = 8 and X = 512, where XSUM as well as X is a cube. Trivial solutions where XSUM as well as X are cubes are X = XSUM = 0 and X = XSUM = 1. Given that there is one more solution where XSUM is a cube than when XSUM is not a cube, how many solutions are there?

Answer, page 75

36. What were the relationships of the people mentioned in the following epitaph?

> Two husbands with their two wives
>
> Two grandmothers with their two granddaughters
>
> Two fathers with their two daughters
>
> Two mothers with their two sons
>
> Two maidens with their two mothers
>
> Two sisters with their two brothers
>
> But only six in all lie buried here
>
> All born legitimate, from incest clear.

Answer, page 69

37. A, B, C, and D each represent a different word or phrase, and they have a common theme. What are the four words or phrases and what is the theme?

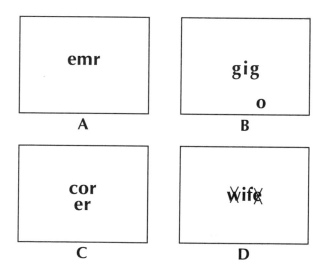

Answer, page 70

38. What three letters should be placed in the three empty circles in order that the longest possible word (which may be more than eight letters long) can be spelled out by reading around the circles? You can choose your starting position and whether to read the letters clockwise or anticlockwise.

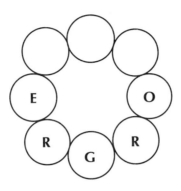

Answer, page 92

39. A carpenter has a solid cube of wood, each edge of which is twelve inches long. He wishes to cut the block in two in such a way that the new face on each of the two pieces can then be trimmed to a square of maximum possible size. Where should he make the cut?

Answer, page 69

40. Each word in the following list is an anagram of a country, but with one letter changed. For example, "least" would lead to "Wales," with "w" replaced by "t." What are the countries?

1. empty

2. tiara

3. tribal

4. warden

5. amenity

6. elegant

7. glacier

8. senator

Answer, page 92

41. Jimmy learned in school that $1^2 + 2^2 = 5$ and $3^2 + 4^2 = 5^2$. Hurrying to do his homework, he writes, $1^3 + 2^3 + 3^3 = 6^2$ and then $3^3 + 4^3 + 5^3 = 6^3$. Was he right?

Answer, page 67

42. Divide the following figure into four parts, with each part being the same size and shape and comprising whole squares only. Each of the four parts should also contain one X and one O, though not necessarily in the same relative positions.

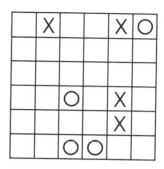

Answer, page 75

43. A, B, C, and D each represent a different word or phrase, and they have a common theme. What are the four words or phrases and what is the theme?

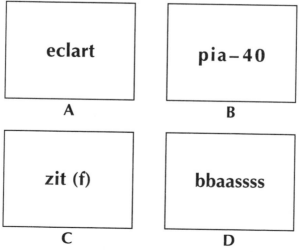

Answer, page 79

44. Triangle OAB is formed by three tangents to a circle with center C. Angle AOB = 40°. What is angle ACB?

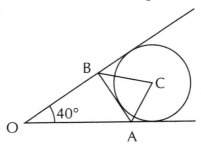

Answer, page 75

45. In the equation below, each letter represents one digit only, and no letter represents the same digit as any other letter:

TIM x SOLE = AMOUNT

Furthermore, and using the same letters to represent the same digits, the difference between LEAST and MOST is ALL. In this puzzle a number may begin with zero; such a zero should be ignored when performing calculations. What digits do the letters stand for?

Answer, page 93

46. Using four 4's, parentheses as necessary, and the following seven symbols as required, find expressions for 73 and 89.

+ − / x . ! √

The use of nonstandard expressions such as .(√4) for 0.2 or (√√√√....√√4) for 1 is not permitted.

Answer, page 77

47. An army four miles long steadily advances four miles while a dispatch rider gallops from the rear to the front, delivers a dispatch to the commanding general as he turns, and gallops back to the rear. How far has the rider traveled?

Answer, page 77

48. A crossword puzzle with some puzzling clues:

ACROSS

1. A kettle called Ronald (8)

3. Divide or add to make her shorter (4)

4. A word that is an anagram of itself (6)

5. An American film actress from Germany (3,4)

6. Contains the letter "e" three times, but often seen containing just one letter (8)

8. ONMLKJIH (9)

DOWN

2. A rope ends it (11)

7. Cheese made backwards (4)

Answer, page 69

49. "Catchphrase" has six consonants in a row and does not have a y. Find a word that starts with seven consonants in a row, counting y as a consonant, and ends with nine.

Answer, page 68

50. A, B, C, and D each represent a different word or phrase, and they have a common theme. What are the four words or phrases and what is the theme?

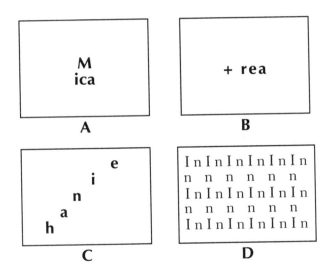

Answer, page 79

51.

If Alan is from New Zealand,

And Britain's where Rita is from,

Please tell me if you are so able,

The countries of Eric and Don?

Answer, page 80

52. **THIS** × **THAT** × **IT** equals a ten-digit number containing each digit once. If each letter represents a different digit, and **THAT** is a perfect square, what is **THIS**?

Answer, page 84

53. What is the missing letter below?

E O E R E X ? T E N

Answer, page 80

54. The hole for letters in the pillar-box at our local post office is rectangular and wider than it is high. Each side of the hole is an integral number of inches in length, and the area of the hole in square inches is 25 percent greater than the perimeter in inches. What is the width of the hole?

Answer, page 76

55. Find an eight-digit number containing eight different digits that is equal to the square of the sum of the number formed by its first four digits and the number formed by its last four digits.

Answer, page 77

56. Jill has thought of a number between 13 and 1,300, and Jack is doing his best to guess it. Unknown to Jack, Jill is not always truthful.

Jack asks whether the number is below 500.	Jill lies.
Jack asks whether the number is a perfect square.	Jill lies.
Jack asks whether the number is a perfect cube.	Jill tells the truth.
Jack then asks whether the second digit is a zero.	Jill answers.

Jack then states the number that he thinks Jill thought of and, not surprisingly, is wrong. From the information above, name Jill's number.

Answer, page 78

57. At work, Alan, Ben, Claire, Dave, Emma, Fiona, Gail, and Henry have their lunch break together. Their lunchroom has four tables against a wall, each for two people.

They decided to have a quiz week where they would each read puzzles over lunch from their favorite puzzle book. In alphabetical order, the eight favorite puzzle books, one per person, were: *Brain Bafflers, Crosswords, Cryptograms, Logic Puzzles, Mazes, Number Games, Probability Paradoxes,* and *Word Search.*

In that week, no two people sat together at lunch more than once. Given that they all lunched together every day unless stated otherwise, determine each person's favorite puzzle book.

Monday

Alan sat beside the reader of *Number Games.*

The *Crosswords* reader was on a diet and skipped the lunch break.

Tuesday

The *Word Search* reader sat beside Gail, and Ben sat beside Emma.

In the evening, Claire left for a week's holiday.

Wednesday

Dave sat beside the *Word Search* reader.

Fiona was ill and so did not go to work that day.

The *Brain Bafflers* reader sat beside Alan, who is not the reader of *Word Search.*

Thursday

The *Mazes* reader was away on business in the morning and missed lunch.

Alan and Emma sat together.

The woman whose favorite puzzle book is *Cryptograms* sat beside Dave.

Friday

Ben took the day off.

Fiona and Dave sat together.

Saturday

The readers of *Number Games* and *Logic Puzzles* sat together.

Answer, page 74

58. A, B, C, and D each represent a different word or phrase, and they have a common theme. What are the four words or phrases and what is the theme?

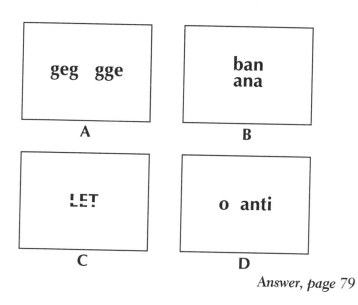

geg gge

A

ban
ana

B

LET

C

o anti

D

Answer, page 79

59. Two pupils were to be chosen at random from a school register to take part in a competition. The probability that both would be boys was one-third. Before the choice could be made however, a decision was taken to include pupils from the register of another school in the ballot for the two places. This other school had a register of 1,000 pupils, and the chance that the two selected pupils would both be boys was reduced to one-thirteenth.

How many pupils are on the register of the first school?

Answer, page 82

60. Punctuate the following so that it makes sense:

Time flies you cannot they go too quickly

Answer, page 79

61. Each clue in this crossword leads to two words that are anagrams of each other. For example, the clue "Drums like the Concorde" would give PERCUSSION/SUPERSONIC. Use interlocking letters to determine which word is to be entered in the diagram.

ACROSS

7. Least colorful parts of a flower (6)

8. Confident save (6)

9. Very odd place for hot coals (7)

11. Subsequently change (5)

12. Provide food for a very small quantity (5)

14. Dependent upon where one finds a relieved soldier? (7)

15. Fired for trying to lose pounds (7)

17. Express reaches the top (5)

20. Applauds the top of the head (5)

21. Place: the upper part (7)

23. Removes more than one case of spots (6)

24. Slip away in a dreamy state (6)

DOWN

1. A type of paper tiger, say (6)

2. Sat down and composed (6)

3. Skills of leading performer (4)

4. Enlarge a small part (6)

5. Most impertinent piece of baggage (8)

6. Got to know regular payment (6)

10. Made furious (7)

13. Produce an adolescent, possibly (8)

15. Came out of obsolescence (6)

16. Make known it may be sweaty (6)

18. Pet dog doubled back (6)

19. Tolerates having prejudice (6)

22. Cheese and wine (4)

Answer, page 82

62. Construct a chess game in which White moves one piece twice and opens with 1. P— KB3 (see diagram), and Black mates on move five with 5. . . . . N x R mate using his king's knight.

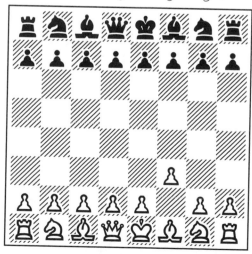

Answer, page 80

63. This is the same as the previous puzzle, but this time the mate in five is with Black's queen's knight.

Answer, page 65

64. Each number from 90 to 99 has been expressed as the product or quotient of two positive integers, neither of which is 1. Each of these integers has, in turn, been expressed as a combination of two integers, and it is these that appear in the diagram below. No number in the diagram begins with 0, and no number appears twice. Capital letters denote "across" numbers, and lowercase letters denote "down" numbers.

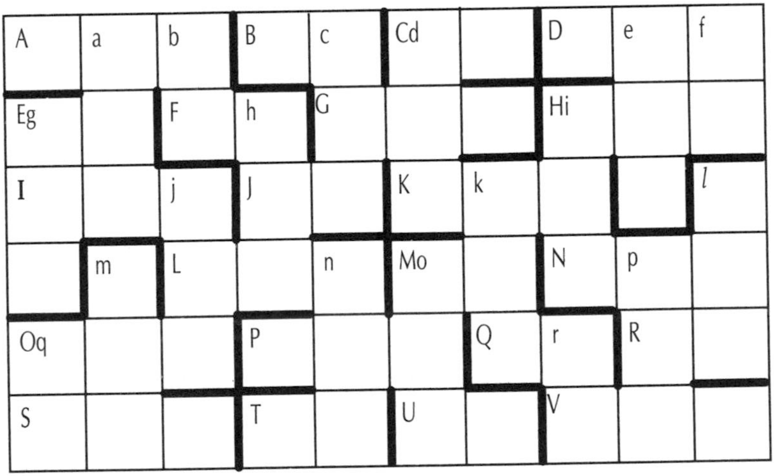

A	a	b	B	c	Cd		D	e	f
Eg		F	h	G			Hi		
I		j	J		K	k			l
	m	L		n	Mo		N	p	
Oq			P			Q	r	R	
S			T		U		V		

$$90 = (A - n) \cdot (H / a)$$
$$91 = (e / E) \cdot (r - F)$$
$$92 = (i \cdot V) / (O \cdot T)$$
$$93 = (g / d) \cdot (o - I)$$
$$94 = (G \cdot p) / (B \cdot l)$$

$$95 = (c - j) \cdot (k - M)$$
$$96 = (D \cdot h) \cdot (K \cdot Q)$$
$$97 = (f \cdot P) / (b - C)$$
$$98 = (J / q) \cdot (N / U)$$
$$99 = (R \cdot S) / (L - m)$$

Answer, page 81

65. In a league of four hockey teams, each team played the other three. After all six games had been played, the following league table was prepared:

Team	Goals	
	For	Against
A	4	0
B	2	1
C	1	3
D	2	5

Team D drew one game and lost its other two. What was the score in each of the six games?

Answer, page 72

66. ABC is an equilateral triangle. Point P within the triangle is six inches from A, eight inches from B, and ten inches from C. What is the area of the triangle?

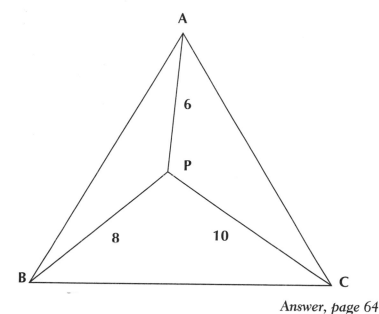

Answer, page 64

67. The answer to the first of these is "24 hours in a day." Complete the rest.

24 H in a D
5 V in the E A
8 L on a S
1,000 W that a P is W
13 S on the A F
14 L in a S
90 D in a R A
9 L of a C

Answer, page 65

68. Benford's Law applies to the terms of the Fibonacci series, the first few of which are shown below:

1   1   2   3   5   8   13   21   34   . . .

That is, the percentage of numbers in the Fibonacci series beginning with the digit N is log $(1 + 1/N) \times 100\%$. Thus, for example, $30.1\% (= \log(2) \times 100\%)$ of the terms in the Fibonacci series begin with a "1." Benford's Law applies to all sorts of other things too, such as share prices, numbers in old magazine articles, and the drainage areas of rivers.

Prove that the percentage of numbers that are predicted to begin with one of the digits between one and nine using the Benford's Law formula total 100%.

Answer, page 66

69. In how many ways can the numbers from 1 to 9 be arranged in a 3 x 3 array, such that no number has a smaller number than itself appearing either immediately below or immediately to the right of it?

Answer, page 66

70. Find a 4 × 4 magic square that contains 16 different integers, each of which is divisible only by itself and one. As a start, one row has already been completed.

As a further hint, the middle four squares have the same total as the rows, columns, and long diagonals.

53	**11**	**37**	**1**

Answer, page 88

71. You have several identical crystals that will shatter if dropped from a certain height or above, but which will remain unscathed if dropped from any height lower than this.

You are in a building that has 106 floors. You have already discovered that a crystal dropped from a window on floor 106 will shatter, but you want to know the lowest floor from which you can drop a crystal so that it will shatter.

You could test one floor at a time starting from floor one, but to save time you want a quicker way than this, so long as no more than two more crystals will be shattered during the testing. From which floor should you make the first drop, and what is the maximum number of drops you will require?

Answer, page 83

72. Using three fours, parentheses where necessary, and the eight symbols below as required, find expressions for 119, 268, and 336.

$$+ \quad - \quad \times \quad / \quad . \quad ! \quad \sqrt{\quad} \quad \Sigma$$

The expression Σn denotes the sum of the first n integers, so $\Sigma 4 = 10$. The use of symbols other than those shown, or nonstandard expressions such as $.(\sqrt{4})$ for 0.2, $.(\Sigma 4)$ for 0.1, or $\sqrt{\sqrt{\sqrt{\sqrt{}}}} ... \sqrt{\sqrt{4}}$ for 1, is not permitted.

Answer, page 84

73. In this crossword, clues are of four different types: synonyms, antonyms, anagrams, and a fourth type that must be determined.

ACROSS

1. Pistol
5. Venomous
10. Pause
11. Coordinate
13. Tear
14. Airs
15. Realize
16. Adze
17. Discern
18. Storm
21. Pleases
24. Dialect
26. Vent
27. Confirm
29. Tail
30. Idol
32. Infidelity
33. Common
34. Patriot
35. Ransom

DOWN

2. Bill
3. Abolish
4. Diet
6. Richest
7. Cater
8. Success
9. Sparing
12. Spoil
16. Young
19. Item
20. Spread
21. Weirdo
22. Bent
23. Sways
24. Urban
25. General
28. Devil
31. Dear

Answer, page 73

74. A New York insurance company has six account managers, each of whom has a different number of children from none to five. Deduce from the following who has what number of children, the account each manages, and where each lives.

1. Angela has two more children than the manager from Manhattan, who has one more child than the fire manager.
2. The marine manager has two more children than the manager from Queens, who has one more child than Enid.
3. The manager from Staten Island has two more children than Dick, who has one more child than the automotive manager.
4. Chloe has three more children than the property manager.
5. The liability manager has more children than the manager from the Bronx, who is not Enid.
6. The manager from Manhattan, who is not the automotive manager, is not Chloe.
7. Enid is not the property manager, and Fred is not the marine manager.
8. The manager from New Jersey may or may not be Brian.
9. The manager from Brooklyn is not the liability manager, but might be the aviation manager.

Answer, page 81

75. A businessman usually travels home each evening on the same train, and his wife leaves home by car just in time to collect him from the station. One day he caught an earlier train, and having forgotten to tell his wife, he walked to meet the car and was then driven straight home, arriving ten minutes earlier than normal.

The businessman's wife drove at a steady 36 mph each way. Had she been a faster driver, averaging 46 mph, then perhaps surprisingly they would have arrived home just eight minutes earlier rather than ten. This is because being a faster driver and planning to arrive at the station at the same time, the wife would have left home later.

How early was the train?

Answer, page 83

76. In this crossnumber puzzle, each number to be entered in the diagram is clued by the number of factors that it has. In this context, both 1 and the number itself are counted as factors. Thus, if 14 were one of the numbers to be entered in the diagram, its clue would be 4, since 14 has four factors (1, 2, 7, and 14).

There is one condition: in the finished diagram, each of the digits from 0 to 9 must appear twice.

Capital letters denote across answers and lowercase letters denote down answers. No answer begins with a zero.

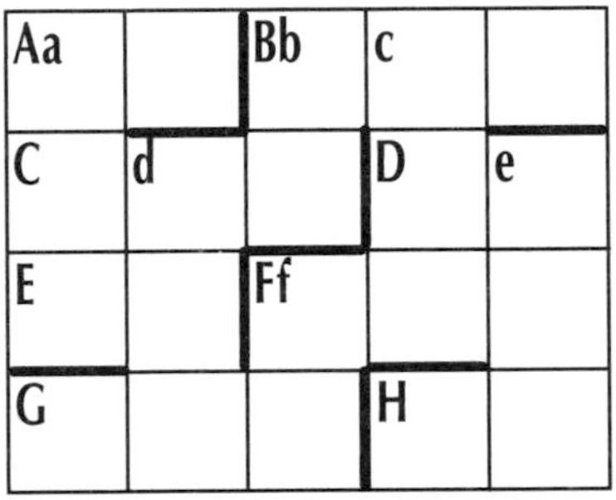

Aa		Bb	c	
C	d		D	e
E		Ff		
G			H	

ACROSS	DOWN
A. 8	a. 15
B. 12	b. 2
C. 2	c. 9
D. 6	d. 18
E. 6	e. 8
F. 24	f. 10
G. 14	
H. 6	

Answer, page 84

77. A, B, C, and D each represent a different word or phrase, and they have a common theme. What are the four words or phrases and what is the theme?

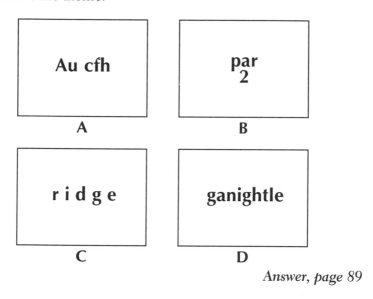

Answer, page 89

78. P and Q are five-digit numbers that between them contain all ten digits, as does their product, P × Q. If P = 54,321, what is Q?

Answer, page 88

79. Tires on Cathy's car last 18,000 miles on the front or 22,000 miles on the back. She has a new set of five tires (including the spare) that she intends to rotate so they can all be replaced at the same time.

A. Assuming no punctures or blowouts, how far can she drive with five tires?

B. Which tires will need to be changed and at what distances if the number of wheel changes she makes is to be kept to a minimum?

Answer, page 77

80. Heather and Lynsey are playing a game of Boxes and have reached the position shown. The object of the game is to complete the most boxes as signified by the initials inside. The rules are that players take turns by adding to the grid a horizontal or vertical line of unit length, and that they have a compulsory extra turn whenever they complete a box. It is Lynsey's turn to play. How can she win?

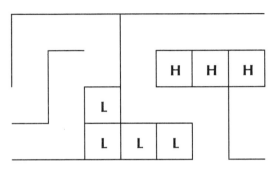

Answer, page 86

81. Samos Farm has four straight sides, and its diagonally opposite corners are joined by two straight roads that run north-south and east-west. The lengths of the sides of the farm and the distances between the crossroads and the four corners are all different, and each is an exact number of chains. (An old-fashioned measure of distance that equals 22 yards.)

Given that one side is 35 chains long and that ten square chains make an acre, what is the farm's area measured in acres?

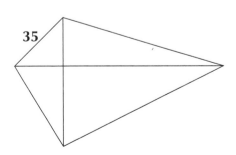

Answer, page 85

82. Here is a "proof" that all triangles are isosceles. Can you spot the flaw?

Begin with any triangle ABC. Let the bisector of angle A meet the perpendicular bisector of BC at O. The diagrams show O inside and outside the triangle, respectively. Let E and F be the feet of the perpendiculars from O to AB and AC.

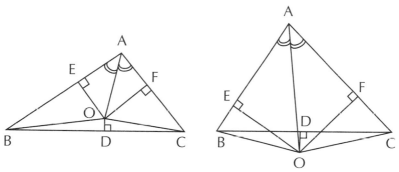

AFO is congruent to AEO, so AE = AF and OE = OF.

BDO is congruent to CDO, so OB = OC.

Thus OEB is congruent to OFC, and EB = FC.

Now, AE = AF and EB = FC, so AE + EB = AF + FC.

Therefore, AB = AC and ABC is isosceles.

Answer, page 91

83. Which two 10-digit numbers, each containing one of each digit, have square roots whose digits are the reverse of one another?

Answer, page 87

84. Find a five-digit palindromic number (a number that equals itself when read backward) that has a remainder of 9 when divided by 10, a remainder of 8 when divided by 9, a remainder of 7 when divided by 8, and so on, and whose digits are all odd.

Answer, page 87

85. The diagram below shows an arrangement of six wooden matches that makes eight triangles.

Without breaking the matches but using lateral thinking, now rearrange the six matches to make eight squares.

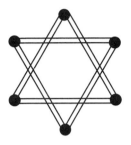

Answer, page 87

86. A, B, C, and D each represent a different word or phrase, and they have a common theme. What are the four words or phrases and what is the theme?

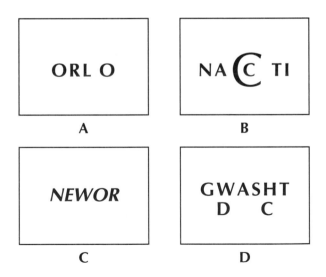

Answer, page 83

87. Place three letters in the three empty circles in order that the longest possible word (which may be more than eight letters long) can be spelled out by reading around the circles. You can choose your starting position and whether to read the letters clockwise or counterclockwise.

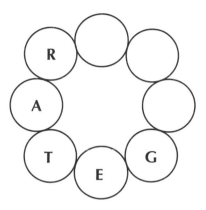

Answer, page 77

88. If Black were to play in the position shown, the game would finish immediately, in stalemate. But White is to play, and he can win in just three moves; how?

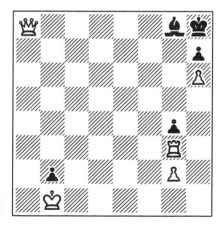

Answer, page 88

89. In this crossnumber puzzle, none of the numbers to be entered in the diagram begins with a zero.

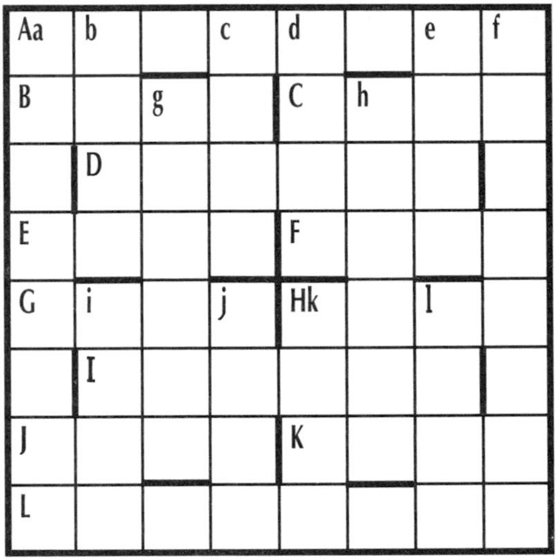

Aa	b		c	d		e	f
B		g		C	h		
	D						
E				F			
G	i		j	Hk		l	
	I						
J				K			
L							

ACROSS

A. Multiple of j
B. Square
C. l − d
D. Fifth power
E. Fourth power
F. Factor of d
G. Square
H. Square
I. Sixth power
J. Multiple of c
K. i − 2b
L. Multiple of E

DOWN

a. c·d
b. Square
c. Square
d. Multiple of F
e. Twice a prime
f. Multiple of j
g. Square
h. Sixth power
i. Prime
j. Cube
k. Square
l. C + d

Answer, page 87

90. Complete the grid using all the letters below so that each row and column containing two or more squares is a word when read from left to right or from top to bottom:

A C C E E E E H L N O W

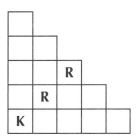

Answer, page 92

91. There are six symmetrical ways in which dots can be placed in 16 different squares in an 8 × 8 array such that every row, column, and diagonal (not just the main diagonals from corner to corner) is either empty or has exactly two dots in it. The solution shown below is one such arrangement, and is also symmetrical when divided in half diagonally from top left to bottom right.

Can you find the one solution (ignoring rotations and reflections) that is not symmetrical?

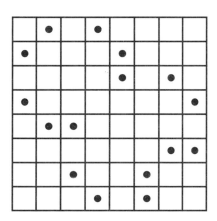

Answer, page 88

92. This crossword—part jigsaw puzzle—is made from the 28 jigsaw pieces shown below. Where some of the letters on the jigsaw pieces should be turned on their side or upside down (because in the jigsaw, the jigsaw piece itself is turned on its side or upside down), the letters have been shown right side up. To avoid giving unneccessary clues, the pieces have been redrawn to a standard shape.

Identify in the completed crossword the exact position of each individual jigsaw piece.

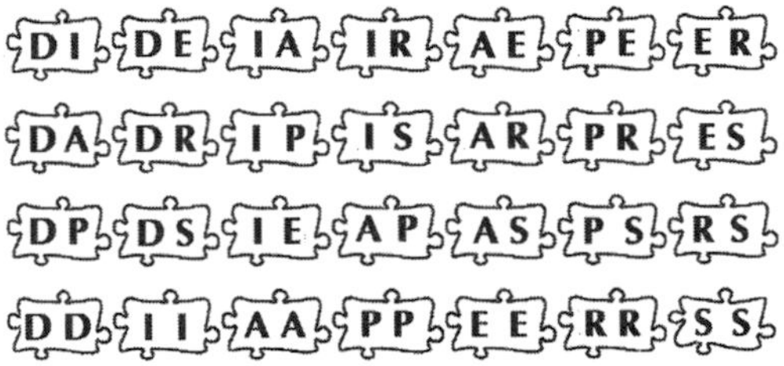

DI DE IA IR AE PE ER
DA DR IP IS AR PR ES
DP DS IE AP AS PS RS
DD II AA PP EE RR SS

1 2 3
4 5 6
7 8 9 10
11
12 13 14
15
16 17

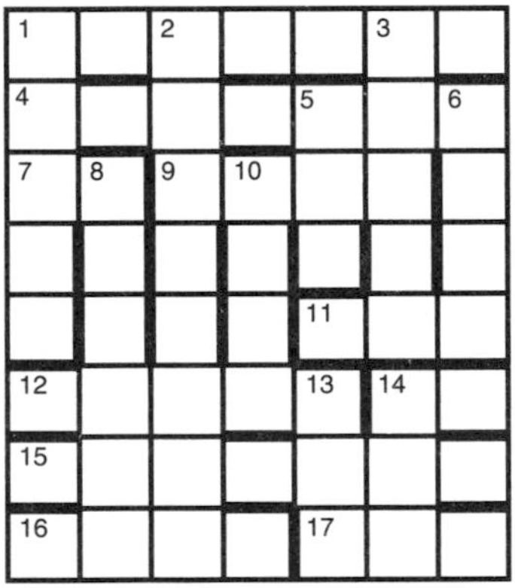

ACROSS

1. Anagram of DIAPERS (7)
4. Another anagram of DIAPERS (7)
7. German villains in Central Russia (2)
9. Raise right, with musical talent (4)
11. Start to play after gym class—it gives you energy (3)
12. Noticed where Pierre is eating dessert (5)
14. The unconscious security guards may ask to see it (2)
15. Another anagram of DIAPERS (7)
16. Caesarean section's region (4)
17. Private eye had backtracked to get pickpocket (3)

DOWN

1. Church areas keep sins from starting (5)
2. Parade is moved to the perfect place (8)
3. Spooky Pennsylvania city makes itself heard (5)
5. In hindsight, that German's upset (3)
6. Dullard to tear after Democrat (4)
8. One who undermines revised papers (6)
10. Gaelic tongue in stanza following introduction (4)
13. By day, spot a close relative (3)
14. Three leaders in Indonesia instigated insurgency (3)

Answer, page 62

93. There are just three clues for this crossnumber:
Every answer is the product of two different primes of equal length.
No answer begins with a zero, and in no answer is a digit repeated.
The digits of the middle six-digit number are in ascending order.

1	2	3	4	5	6
7					
8					
9					
		10			

Answer, page 89

94. There was a group of three men. When asked a question, one of the men would always answer truthfully, one would always lie, and the third would lie at random. They know who has which habit, but you do not.

How, in only three questions to which the man being asked can only answer "yes" or "no," can you discover which man has which habit? Each of the three questions can be put to one man only, but it need not be to the same man each time. For example, questions one and two could go to the first man, and question three to the second.

Answer, page 87

95. A rectangular cake is being baked to meet the following requirements:

- The cake can be cut into five rectangular pieces such that each piece has sides that are a whole number of inches long, and
- Sides of the pieces and sides of the original cake all have different measurements.

What is the area of the smallest cake that will meet these requirements?

Answer, page 90

96. A, B, C, and D each represent a different word or phrase, and they have a common theme. What are the four words or phrases and what is the theme?

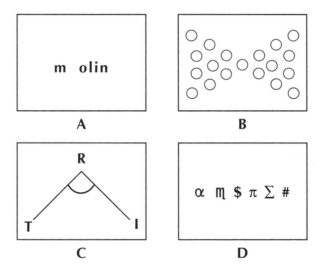

A   B

C   D

Answer, page 92

97. What property having to do with factorials makes the number 145 interesting?

Answer, page 92

98. Each empty square in this grid is to be filled with a single letter. When read consecutively, the 18 letters spell out a well-known object.

The numbers between the letters provide the only clues. Letting A = 1, B = 2, up to Z = 26, each number indicates the difference between the adjacent letter values. For example, 4 could separate E and A, B and F, and so on. What is the object?

	12		3		14		1		19	
0		13		0		4		14		11
	1		16		10		9		6	
11		19		0		3		14		13
	7		3		13		2		5	

Answer, page 78

99.

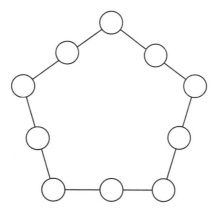

A. Arrange the digits from 0 to 9 in the circles around the pentagon in such a way that the three numbers on each side of the pentagon add up to eleven.

B. Now rearrange the digits in such a way that, starting from a suitable side and moving clockwise, the sums on successive sides are consecutive integers, none of which equals eleven.

Answer, page 84

100. There are nine indistinguishable mince pies. Some mincemeat has been removed from one, chosen at random, and put back in another pie, also chosen at random. Thus, either one pie is light and another heavy by the same amount, or else they all have the same weight.

With four trials using a simple balance, either establish that all mince pies have the same weight or identify the light and heavy ones.

Answer, page 78

101. What two-word phrase could form the first and fourth rows of the diagram, so that each column contains a five-letter word?

U	V	A	L	O
M	E	S	A	D
Y	T	S	E	L

Answer, page 67

102. If all you knew about Britney Spears was that her name was an anagram of "best in prayers," why might you think her parents were not Catholics? (Hint: look for another anagram, this time one word of thirteen letters.)

Answer, page 69

103. David's mother has three children. She also has three coins from the United States and decides to give one to each child.

Penelope is given a penny.

Nicholas is given a nickel.

What is the name of the child who gets the dime?

Answer, page 68

104. The number 153 is interesting for two reasons. The first has something to do with factorials, and the second has to do with cubes. What are these two reasons, and what other three-digit number shares the second property?

Answer, page 66

105. A, B, C, and D each represent a different word or phrase, and they have a common theme. What are the four words or phrases and what is the theme?

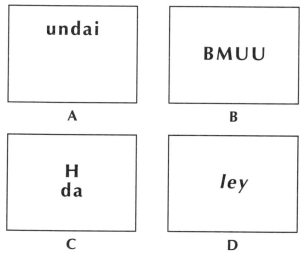

106. Arrange six matches in such a way that each one touches four of the other five.

Answer, page 85

107. If W = 2, U = 4, V = 5, G = 8, and Y = 20, what does D equal?

Answer, page 83

108. Seven friends stranded on a desert island start arguing about what day of the week it is.

Andrew thinks that yesterday was Wednesday.

Dave disagrees, saying that tomorrow is Wednesday.

John maintains that the day after tomorrow is Tuesday.

Pete feels sure that yesterday was not Friday.

Fred believes that today is Tuesday.

Mick says that today is not Sunday, Monday, or Tuesday.

Charlie is adamant that it is Tuesday tomorrow.

If just one of them is right, what day of the week is it?

Answer, page 88

109. Which five of these six pieces can be arranged to form a 5 × 5 checkerboard pattern?

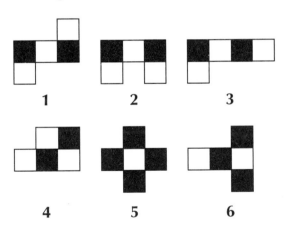

Answer, page 67

110. How should the digits from one to eight be arranged as two four-digit numbers so that the product of the two numbers is (**a**) a minimum and (**b**) a maximum?

Answer, page 72

111. Place a letter in each of the ten spaces such that:

• Five six-letter words, including one country, are formed by reading in a straight line from each of five letters in the outer ring to the ones at the opposite side, and

• The ten letters in the middle circle, read clockwise, spell out the name of another country.

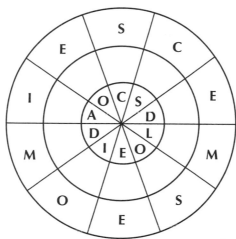

Answer, page 92

112. Four women weighed 105, 110, 115, and 120 pounds, respectively. Two weeks ago, Carol announced that she was going on a diet, and the other three immediately decided to join her.

Since starting the diet, no woman's weight has changed by more than five pounds, and all weights are still whole numbers of pounds. Debbie has lost more weight than Miss Easton. Anne weighed ten pounds more than Debbie when they started the diet. Miss Green now weighs ten pounds less than Miss Hope. Miss Frost now weighs seven pounds less than Barbara did before dieting. Miss Hope actually put on weight, but still weighs less than Anne. Barbara has lost more weight than Anne. Miss Easton now weighs four pounds more than Anne.

What are the names and current weights of the four women?

Answer, page 90

113. The segment below is one-sixth of a circle. Dots A and B on the arc divide that arc into thirds. The other two dots, C and D, are two-thirds of the way from the nearest part of the arc to what would have been the center of the circle.

Are the lines AC and BD parallel? If not, on which side of the segment would they meet if they were extended?

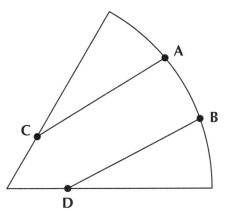

Answer, page 89

114. What number should replace the question mark in the following array?

1	2	3	4	5
1	3	9	21	41
1	4	31	220	1,081
1	5	129	6,949	?

Answer, page 64

115. In a certain fashion show, the exhibits included 36 outfits by Jasper Conran, 35 by Calvin Klein, and 56 by Yves Saint-Laurent. How many outfits did Vivienne Westwood exhibit?

Answer, page 89

116. Place the numbers from one to eight in the grid in such a way that each number differs from its neighbors horizontally, vertically, and diagonally by at least two.

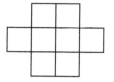

Answer, page 90

117. In this magic square, A, B, and C are single-digit numbers, 2A means twice A, and so on. Every row, column, and both diagonals add up to the same total. What is that total?

2A	C	2C
A+2B	A+B	A
B	3A	2B

Answer, page 91

118. A secretary was asked to organize a mailing to a 10% sample of a company's clients. Rather than just pick 10% of the clients on his mailing list randomly, however, the secretary decided to pick the first client, skip one, pick the next, skip two, pick the next, skip three, pick the next, and so on, until he came to the end of the list. To his surprise, the final client that he picked happened to be the last one on the mailing list. Moreover, as required, he had picked exactly 10% of the total.

How many names were on the mailing list?

Answer, page 90

119. On a regular 8 × 8 chessboard, shown below, only five queens are needed in order to ensure that all unoccupied squares are attacked.

How many queens are needed on an 11 × 11 board?

Answer, page 79

120. The diagram below shows five flat interlocked rings lying on the ground. Four are made of a rigid metal; the fifth is made of rubber. Which is the rubber one?

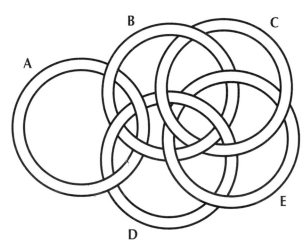

Answer, page 75

121. One leaf has been torn out of a book. The sum of the remaining page numbers is 10,000. What is the last-numbered page in the book, and which leaf is missing?

Answer, page 80

122. The piece below on the left comprises three squares of unit length. What is the smallest rectangle that can be covered with pieces of this shape in a way such that no two pieces form a 2 × 3 rectangle (as shown below on the right)?

Answer, page 72

123. The diagram below shows two railway lines with a crossover track. The task for the two engine drivers is to exchange the two wagons on the top track with the two on the bottom track, with the wagons finishing in the same order from left to right as they started. What makes the task difficult is that the usable stretch of straight track at the bottom right will take only two wagons, while the usable stretch at the top right will take only two wagons and an engine. How can the drivers accomplish the task?

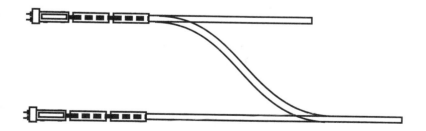

Answer, page 71

124. I ordered four items, the prices of which were $27, $34, $84, and $91. When I went to pay for them, I discovered my son had also ordered one of these items and, quite independently, so had his wife. To save time, I decided to pay for all six items.

Explaining this to the cashier seemed to put him in a state of confusion, because he then entered every price with its digits reversed— so that $27 was entered as $72, for example. However, by a remarkable coincidence, the total turned out to be correct anyway.

How much between them do my son and his wife owe me?

Answer, page 90

125. What three letters should be placed in the three empty circles so that the longest possible word (which may be more than eight letters long) can be spelled out by reading around the circles? You can choose your starting position and whether to read the letters clockwise or counter clockwise.

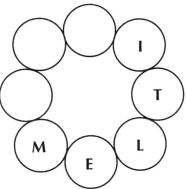

Answer, page 80

126. Emma buys seven items. The prices of the items are all different, and the total cost is $10.71. Emma checks this on her calculator, but inadvertently multiplies the amounts together instead of adding. The result, with correct treatment of decimal points, is also $10.71. What are the prices of the seven items?

Answer, page 88

127. A construction worker was asked to dig a ditch into which a 9" diameter pipe would be laid. He dug a triangular ditch with an angle of 60° to a depth of 12", but as the cross-section shows, this was not deep enough to hide the whole pipe below the surface.

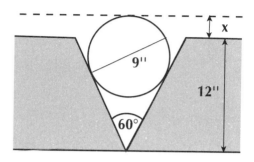

How far above the surface — the distance marked x in the diagram — does the pipe protrude?

Answer, page 68

128. In what way are the letters in the top row different from the letters in the bottom row?

C	I	O	Q	U
B	P	R	T	Y

Answer, page 92

129. An old adage describes how an explorer, lost in strange territory, set out from her camp, walked a mile south, then a mile east, and then a mile north and found herself back at her camp looking at a bear. The question is then: "What color is the bear?" The answer to this conundrum is "white" because the explorer was at the North Pole, but could the explorer have been anywhere else? If so, where?

Answer, page 92

130. A, B, C, and D each represent a different word or phrase, and they have a common theme. What are the four words or phrases and what is the theme?

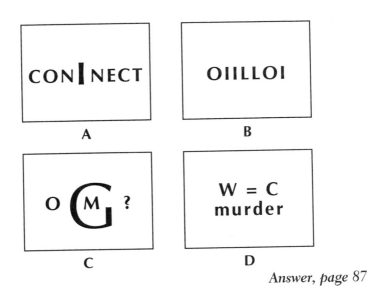

A

B

C

D

Answer, page 87

131. Using the integers 1 to 49, construct a 7 × 7 grid where every row, every column, and the two major diagonals add up to 175 (a 7 × 7 magic square), and the grid contains a 5 × 5 and a 3 × 3 magic square.

A start is given in the diagram below.

10						
	19					
		24				
			25			
				26		
					31	
						40

Answer, page 81

132. Three children of different ages share the same birthday. On one of their birthdays, one of their ages was the sum of the other two ages. On another birthday a few years later, the youngest observed that one of their ages was half the sum of the other two ages. When the number of years since the first occasion was half the sum of the ages on the first occasion, one celebrated her 18th birthday. What birthdays were the other two celebrating at this time?

Answer, page 69

133. Which is capable of filling more of the available space—a square peg in a round hole or a round peg in a square hole?

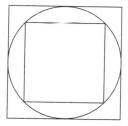

Answer, page 70

134. In this multiplication problem, each digit appears once and once only (so each "×" represents a different digit), and the three-digit number is prime. What are the two numbers that are being multiplied together?

$$\begin{array}{r} \text{X X X} \\ \times \text{ X X} \\ \hline \text{X X X X X} \end{array}$$

Answer, page 80

135. Flying over a plantation, the pilot looks down and announces that he can see six rows of four trees. "So that is 24 trees?" his passenger asks. "Actually no," says the pilot, "just half that number."

In what pattern are the trees planted?

Answer, page 65

ANSWERS

92.

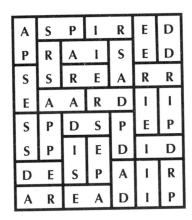

Some of the clues explained:

7 Across   The SS were German villains, and the letters SS
           are found in the center of the word "Russia."

9 Across   To raise a child is to REAR a child; right is R, and
           someone with musical talent has a good ear.

11 Across   PE (gym class), followed by the first letter of "play," gives you PEP.

12 Across   South Dakota (or SD, for short) is where Pierre is, and if you put pie (dessert) inside, you get SPIED.

14 Across   The id is the unconscious; security guards may ask to see your ID.

16 Across   AREA (region) is contained as a section of the word "Caesarean."

17 Across   "PI'd" reversed gives you DIP.

1 Down   If you keep "lapses" (sins) from starting, you get APSES.

2 Down   "Parade is" anagrams to PARADISE.

3 Down   Erie, Pennsylvania is a homophone of EERIE.

5 Down   "Das" is German for "that"; in hindsight (that is, read backwards), it's SAD.

6 Down   To tear is to rip, D is short for Democrat, and a dullard is a DRIP.

8 Down   To sap is to undermine, so one who undermines is a SAPPER, which is an anagram of "papers."

10 Down   A stanza is a verse; following the introduction of that word is ERSE, which is a Gaelic language.

13 Down   D stands for day, and a spot is an advertisement (or, more briefly, an ad), giving DAD.

14 Down   The initial letters of "Indonesia instigated insurgency" spell III.

66. The area of triangle ABC is $(25\sqrt{3} + 36)$ inches². To show this, consider any two of the triangles making up the equilateral triangle, say ABP and ACP (shown as ACP'). Place the two triangles together, AB on AC, to obtain the figure shown:

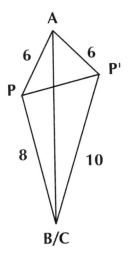

Angles PAB and CAP' total 60°, so PAP' is equilateral. Hence the quadrilateral APBP' can be regarded as an equilateral triangle with 6-inch sides on top of a right-angled triangle with sides 6, 8, and 10 inches. The overall area of the quadrilateral is therefore $(9\sqrt{3} + 24)$ inches².

By taking ABP and BCP, and ACP and BCP, other quadrilaterals can be constructed in a similar manner. Their areas are $(16\sqrt{3} + 24)$ inches² and $(25\sqrt{3} + 24)$ inches² respectively.

The total area of the three quadrilaterals so constructed is $(50\sqrt{3} + 72)$ inches². Because this counts each triangle within the original triangle twice, the area of triangle ABC is therefore $(25\sqrt{3} + 36)$ inches².

114. The missing number is 244,769. This is calculated by adding the number to its left to the product of the two numbers above them. In this case, $6{,}949 + 1{,}081 \times 220$. An example from the grid is $220 = 31 + 21 \times 9$.

67. 24 hours in a day
5 vowels in the English alphabet
8 legs on a spider
1,000 words that a picture is worth
13 stripes on the American flag
14 lines in a sonnet
90 degrees in a right angle
9 lives of a cat

63.

WHITE	BLACK
1. P—KB3	N—QR3
2. P—QR4	N—N5
3. P—Q4	P—QB3
4. R—R3	Q—R4
5. R—Q3	N x R mate

The diagram shows the mate.

135. The trees are planted as follows:

```
      X           X

      X   X   X   X

      X   X   X   X

      X           X
```

69. The number of possible arrangements is 42. To prove this, note that the positions of the 1 and the 9 are fixed. Now suppose that the 2 is placed below the 1. Then if the 3 is placed below the 2, five arrangements are possible. Alternatively, if the 3 is placed to the right of the 1, then there are five arrangements with the 4 under the 2, five with the 5 under the 2, four with the 6 under the 2, and two with the 7 under the 2. This gives a total of 21 arrangements. But by symmetry we would have another 21 if we had started by placing the 2 to the right of the 1, which gives a grand total of 42. (Notice that the digit in the center must be the 4, 5, or 6.)

104. $153 = 1! + 2! + 3! + 4! + 5!$ and $153 = 1^3 + 5^3 + 3^3$. Also, $371 = 3^3 + 7^3 + 1^3$.

5. One solution is shown in the diagram.

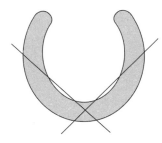

The second solution is to cut the horseshoe into three pieces with one cut, and then put them on top of one another for the next cut. The third solution is to cut the horseshoe in half along the plane of the page, and leaving these pieces on top of one another, cut each of these two pieces into three pieces.

68.

$$\text{Let } V = [\log (1 + 1/1) + \log (1 + 1/2) + \log (1 + 1/3) + \dots + \log (1 + 1/9)] \times 100\%$$
$$\text{Then } V = [\log (2/1) + \log (3/2) + \log (4/3) + \dots + \log (10/9)] \times 100\%$$
$$= [\log (2/1 \times 3/2 \times 4/3 \times \dots \times 10/9)] \times 100\%$$
$$= [\log (10)] \times 100\%$$
$$= 100\%$$

41.   Luckily for Jimmy, yes!

15.   A = buttercup; B = rose (homophone of rows); C = ivy (the clue is in roman numerals); D = hyacinth (high "a," "c" in "th"). The theme is plants.

7.   Our answer is "United States."

12.   29 days in February in a leap year
    12 signs of the zodiac
    7 wonders of the ancient world
    54 cards in a deck (with the jokers)
    32 degrees Fahrenheit, at which water freezes
    18 holes on a golf course
    4 quarts in a gallon
    14 pounds in a stone

109.   The easiest way to solve this puzzle is to note that the 5 × 5 checkerboard must have 13 squares of one color and 12 of the other. Now, if the cross-shaped piece is excluded, the remaining five pieces comprise 14 white and 11 black squares. Thus the cross-shaped piece must be used.

It is then not too difficult to find the following solution (piece 1 is not used):

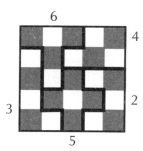

18.   Hawaii is the southernmost state and Alaska the northernmost and westernmost state. Less obviously, Alaska is also the easternmost state of the U.S.A. This is on account of the Aleutian Islands, which extend from the southwest corner of Alaska's mainland across the line of longitude 180° E/W.

101.   Our answer is "Booby prize."

127. Construct a line from O, the center of the pipe, to the foot of the ditch, C, and a radius from O to where the pipe touches one side of the ditch at A. Angle OCA = 60°/2 = 30°, so angle AOC = 60°. Let B be the point where OC crosses the pipe.

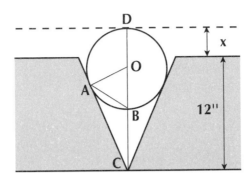

Angle AOB = 60° and OA = OB, so AOB is equilateral and BA = OB = 4.5".

Since angle OAC = 90° and angle OAB = 60°, then angle BAC = 30°.

Thus, BAC is isosceles and BC = BA = OB = 4.5".

DC = DO + OB + BC = 4.5" + 4.5" + 4.5" = (12 + x)".

Thus x, the amount the pipe protrudes above the ground, is 1.5".

103. David, of course. Read the question!

49. Strychnine.

6. A = eyes; B = mouth; C = foot; D = spine. The theme is parts of the body.

16. The two lists of words, with the reinserted letters shown uppercase, were as follows: Ado, eBb, CoDE, siFt, Gel, HeIr, JoKe, LuMiNOus, Pig, QuaRtS, TUg, liVe, WaXY, Zest; and doZe, boY, siX, tWelVe, rUT, SoRe, QuiP, ONus, MiLK, JIg, HuG, FatE, gliDe, CaB, eAst.

Minor variations are possible. For example, in the first set of words, "CoDEs, Fit" could replace "CoDE, siFt."

14. 2,025 or 3,025, as $(30 + 25)^2 - (20 + 25)^2 = 3,025 - 2,025 = 1,000$

132. The birthdays being celebrated were 12, 15, and 18. On the first occasion the birthdays being celebrated were 3, 6, and 9. On every birthday the middle child has an age that is half the sum of the other two ages.

39. The position for the cut of the block is shown in the diagram. The side of the cut square is $\sqrt{9^2 + 9^2}$ inches $= \sqrt{(12^2 + 3^2 + 3^2)}$ inches, which is approximately 12.7 inches.

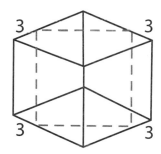

36. Two unrelated women each married the other's son from a previous marriage. Each couple then had a daughter.

102. Britney Spears is an anagram of Presbyterians.

19 . One solution is for the digits 0, 1, 2, 3, 4 and 5 to appear on cube one and the digits 0, 1, 2, 6, 7 and 8 to appear on cube two. For dates that include the number 9, simply turn the 6 upside down.

48. Across: 1. Cauldron, 3. Sort, 4. Stifle, 5. Meg Ryan, 6. Envelope, 8. Backwater (O to II is H_2O backwards). Down: 2. Desperation, 7. Edam.

13	**NAME**	Mr. Gray	Mr. Brown	Mr. Green	Mr. Black	Mr. White
	HOUSE	Blue	Maroon	Mauve	Yellow	Red
	TOWN	Wagga Wagga	Woy Woy	Bong Bong	Peka Peka	Aka Aka
	TEAM	Waratahs	Brumbies	Sharks	Hurricanes	Crusaders
	PET	Kangaroo	Koala	Kookaburra	Kiwi	Kea

Antipodeans may recognize that those who come from Australia have Australian pets and support Australian rugby teams, whereas Mr. White and Mr. Black, the two New Zealanders, have New Zealand pets and support New Zealand rugby teams.

133. A round peg will fill a maximum of $\pi/4 = 78.5\%$ of a square hole. A round hole of unit radius can contain a square peg of maximum side $\sqrt{2}$, and so the square peg will fill a maximum of $2/\pi = 63.7\%$ of a round hole.

Thus the round peg in a square hole is the better fit.

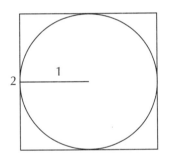 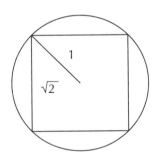

37. A = miner; B = gigolo; C = coroner; D = midwife. The theme is jobs.

25. Each number is put in a column according to the number of letters it has when it is written as a word. The first column contains all the numbers with three letters, the second column has all the numbers with four letters, and so on.

    A. 11 and 12 each have six letters when written as words, and so would appear in the fourth column.

    B. The final entry in the third column would be 60.

20. A = Bronx; B = Broadway; C = Central Park; D = Times Square. The theme is New York City.

31.

N	N	F	X	I	S
E	E	I	O	W	T
I	V	V	N	U	H
G	E	E	E	E	R
H	S	Z	T	L	E
T	W	E	L	V	E

21. True. A tube designed to hold four tennis balls will be half full with two tennis balls and still half full with three tennis balls. This is because the volume of three tennis balls of unit radius is $3 \times 4/3\pi = 4\pi$ cubic units, which is half the volume of a cylinder of unit radius and eight units (four tennis balls) high.

123. Labeling the engines, wagons, and different parts of the track as shown will make the solution given here (there is at least one other) easier to follow:

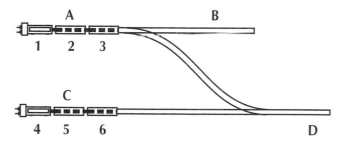

Move 123 to B and uncouple 3. Return 12 to A.
Move 456 to D and uncouple 5 and 6.
Move 12 toward D and couple with 5. Return 125 to A.
Move 125 to B, uncouple 5 and return 12 to A.
Move 12 toward D, leaving 2 in D, where it is picked up by 4 and taken to C.
1 picks up 5 and 3 from B and leaves 3 in D.
42 picks up 3 and returns to C.
Finally 15 picks up 6 from D and returns to A.

110. (A) $1,357 \times 2,468 = 3,349,076$
(B) $8,531 \times 7,642 = 65,193,902$

28. Yes, one, nine, three, nine, three, and nine.

23. Across: 1. Postponed, 3. Other, 4. Astronomer, 5. HMS Pinafore, 6. Endearments, 7. A shoplifter, 8. The eyes. Down: 2. The countryside.

122. Apart from its mirror image, the four-by-six solution below is unique.

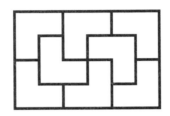

65. D scored no goals against A, and at most one goal against B.
D scored two goals in total, but did not win a game, so D's score against C was 1:1.
D drew against C and so lost to B, so D's score against B was 1:2.
All of B's goals, for and against, were in its match against D, so B's games with A and C were both 0:0.
By subtraction, A's scores against both C and D were 2:0.
The results are summarized below:

A vs B	0:0
A vs C	2:0
A vs D	2:0
B vs C	0:0
B vs D	2:1
C vs D	1:1

27. One, one, nine, three, and nine.

30. A = pony; B = dingo; C = sheep; D = lioness. The theme is animals.

73. The fourth clue type is homophones.

1	2	3	4	5	6	7	8	9	10	11	12	13	14	15
S	P	O	I	L	T	▮	S	P	I	T	E	F	U	L
▮	L	▮	N	I	▮	▮	O	▮	R	▮	A	▮	▮	E
P	A	W	S	▮	D	E	C	O	R	A	T	I	O	N
▮	C	▮	T	I	E	R	▮	R	▮	C	▮	L	▮	I
S	A	R	I	▮	O	▮	E	X	E	C	U	T	E	E
▮	R	▮	T	▮	A	D	D	S	▮	R	▮	▮	▮	N
A	D	J	U	D	G	E	▮	T	E	M	P	E	S	T
▮	T	▮	E	▮	▮	▮	▮	▮	M	▮	L	▮	▮	▮
O	F	F	E	N	D	S	C	I	T	A	D	E	L	▮
D	▮	A	▮	E	X	I	T	▮	S	▮	▮	N	▮	▮
D	E	C	L	A	R	E	▮	V	▮	T	A	L	E	▮
B	▮	U	▮	S	▮	▮	I	D	L	E	▮	▮	A	▮
A	L	L	E	G	I	A	N	C	E	▮	R	A	R	E
L	▮	T	▮	E	▮	W	▮	E	▮	▮	R	E	G	▮
L	O	Y	A	L	I	S	T	▮	R	E	D	E	E	M

33. Yes, but only in the sense that the letters in each word are in alphabetical order.

22. The numbers correspond to the alphabetical positions of the letters I, V, X, L, D and M; that is, the letters which are used in Roman numerals written in ascending order of value. The missing letter is "C", which in this sequence corresponds to 3.

32. Mozambique.

2. One set of solutions is:
   1. Decade   2. Emblem   3. Sheepish   4. Headache
   5. Church   6. Legible   7. Periscope   8. Keepsake

34. It is not possible to end up with just one peg on the board if the central hole starts off empty. To show this, label the holes as shown:

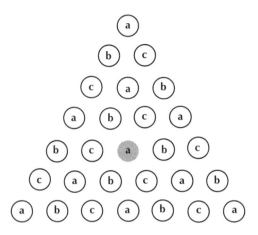

Initially there are nine pegs of each letter. After any move, the number of pegs in two of a, b, and c will be reduced by one, and the number of pegs in the holes of the remaining letter will be increased by one. Thus, at any stage, the amount of pegs assigned to each letter will be either all odd or all even. Hence it is impossible to be left with only one peg on the board, for this would require an odd number (namely one) of pegs in holes of one particular letter and an even number (namely zero) of pegs in the holes of the two other letters.

57. The favorite puzzle books were:

Alan	*Probability Paradoxes*	Emma	*Logic Puzzles*
Ben	*Brain Bafflers*	Fiona	*Mazes*
Claire	*Crosswords*	Gail	*Cryptograms*
Dave	*Number Games*	Henry	*Word Search*

11. A = Top Gun; B = Terms of Endearment; C = Born on the Fourth of July (the "y" is the fourth letter of "July"); D = Men in Black. The theme is films.

35. The seven solutions are: 0/0, 1/1, 8/512, 17/4,913, 18/5,832, 26/17,576, and 27/19,683. The four solutions where XSUM is a cube are: 0, 1, 8 and 27.

Note that XSUM = 64 = 4^3 cannot be a solution as X would then need to be at least an eight-digit number, yet 64^3 is only a six-digit number.

42.

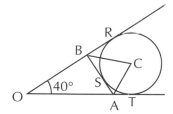

120. Ring D goes over B, which goes over A, which goes over D. Thus, the rubber ring must be A, B, or D. Similarly, B goes over C, which goes over E, which goes over B. The common ring in each case is B, so it must be the rubber one.

1. A = Adam; B = Joseph; C = Richard; D = Justin. The theme is boys' names.

44.

Angle O = 40°, so angles OAB + OBA = 180°− 40°= 140°
Angle TAS = 180°− angle OAB
Angle RBS = 180°− angle OBA
So angles TAS + RBS = 360°− 140°= 220°.
Since CA and CB bisect angles TAS and RBS, respectively,
    angles CAS + CBS = 110°.
Thus, angle ACB = 180°− 110°= 70°.
This angle is independent of the position of the tangent ASB.

3. The semicircle and the tetrahedron are the next two shapes in the series.

The six shapes are a cube, prism, circle, hexagon, cylinder, and rectangle. The number of letters in the name increases by one each time, from four to nine. Of the four shapes from which the seventh and eighth can be chosen, namely a square, tetrahedron, semicircle, and pyramid, only the semicircle and tetrahedron have 10 and 11 letters, respectively.

29.

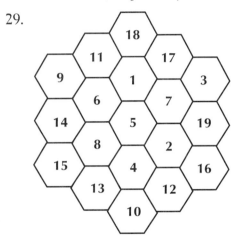

54. Let the dimensions of the hole be x by y inches, then: $1.25(2x + 2y) = xy$, from which $xy - 2.5x - 2.5y = 0$. This may be expressed as $(x - 2.5)(y - 2.5) = 6.25$.

The only integral solutions to this equation are $x = y = 5$, and $x = 15$ and $y = 3$ (or vice versa). Because the hole is wider than it is high, we require the latter solution, so the width of the hole for the letters is 15 inches.

4. Prime numbers of more than one digit end with 1, 3, 7, or 9, as do numbers that are three times prime numbers of more than one digit. Neither the third nor sixth digit of the required ten-digit number can be 7, and 9 cannot appear anywhere in the number. Knowing these facts helps narrow down the possibilities. The required number is 2,412,134,003.

55. 60,481,729, which is $(6{,}048 + 1{,}729)^2 = 7{,}777^2$.

46. $73 = \left(\sqrt{\sqrt{\sqrt{4}}}\right)^{4!} + \dfrac{4}{.\dot{4}}$ and $89 = \left(4!/\sqrt{.\dot{4}} - .4\right)/.4$

A dot over a decimal indicates that it is a repeating decimal.

79. A. The tire wear after 1,000 miles will be: $1/18 + 1/18 + 1/22 + 1/22 = 20/99$ of a tire. Five tires will therefore last $99/20 \times 5 \times 1{,}000$ miles $= 24{,}750$ miles.

B. Four changes are needed, as shown below:

Miles	Front left	Front right	Rear left	Rear right	Spare
0–6,750	A	B	C	D	E
6,750–11,000	A	E	C	D	B
11,000–13,750	A	E	C	B	D
13,750–18,000	A	E	D	B	C
18,000–24,750	C	E	D	B	A

87. Starting with the lower right empty circle and reading counterclockwise, enter the letters "i," "s," and "t" so that "strategist" can be spelled out.

47. Suppose the army has advanced x miles before the commanding general receives the dispatch. The dispatch rider will then have ridden x + 4 miles.

The dispatch rider now rides $(x + 4) - 4 = x$ miles back to where the army commenced its advance. The rider will arrive at this point at the same time as the rear of the army does and when the front of the army completes its 4 miles advance. Thus, the rider travels $2x + 4$ miles while the army travels 4 miles.

Assuming constant speeds throughout, the ratio of the dispatch rider's speed to the army's speed will also be constant. Thus:

$$\frac{x + 4}{x} = \frac{2x + 4}{4}$$

from which $4x + 16 = 2x^2 + 4x$ and $x = \sqrt{8}$.

The dispatch rider travels $4 + 2x$ miles $= 9.66$ miles.

100.   One solution is to weigh 1 + 2 + 3 against 4 + 5 + 6, and 1 + 5 + 7 against 2 + 4 + 8, 1 + 4 against 2 + 5, and 3 + 6 against 7 + 8. From the results of these four weighings, it can be ascertained which, if any, are the lighter and heavier mince pies.

56.   If Jill had said that the number was neither a perfect square nor perfect cube, then Jack would not have had enough information for an answer. Therefore, Jill must have said that the number was a square or a cube or both. The table below shows the possibilities:

Range	Squares	Cubes	Both
13–499	16, 25, 36, 49, 64, 81,	27, 64	64
	100, 121, 144, 169, 196,	125	
	225, 256, 289, 324, 361,	216	
	400, 441, 484	343	
500–1,300	529, 576, 625, 676, 729,	512	729
	784, 841, 900, 961, 1,024,	729	
	1,089, 1,156, 1,225, 1,296	1,000	

Jill could not have said that the number was a perfect square and a perfect cube; otherwise, Jack could have guessed the number after three questions.

If Jill had said that the number was a perfect square but not a perfect cube, then the fourth question would not have been sufficient to identify the number.

If Jill had said that the number was a perfect cube but not a perfect square, then the fourth question would have been sufficient to identify the number (512 or 1,000) only if Jill had said that the number was not below 500.

Jill therefore answered that the number was not below 500, was not a perfect square, but was a perfect cube. This tells us that the number is below 500, is a perfect square, and is a perfect cube. Therefore, Jill's number is 64.

98.   The Statue of Liberty.

58. A = scrambled eggs; B = banana split; C = cutlet; D = antipasto. The theme is food.

119. Remarkably, five queens are still sufficient.

43. A = clarinet; B = pianoforte; C = zither; D = double bass. The theme is musical instruments.

9.

D			
I	F		
S	E	A	
C	E	N	T

60. Time flies? You cannot—they go too quickly. (If the meaning is still not apparent, "time" is used as a verb and "flies" as a noun.)

10. Across: 2. Parishioners, 3. Point, 4. Past due, 5. An aisle, 6. The Morse code, 7. Twelve + One, 8. Arguments. Down: 1. The nudist colony.

24. A = The Fifth Element; 13 = What Lies Beneath; C – Ghostbusters; D = Braveheart. The theme is films.

50. A = Monica; B = Andrea; C = Stephanie; D = Ingrid. The theme is girls' names.

121. The last-numbered page in the book is number 141, and the missing leaf contains pages 5 and 6. Note that the seemingly alternative solution of the last-numbered page being 142 and the missing leaf being pages 76 and 77 does not work. This is because page 76 would be on the left and page 77 on the right, and therefore on different leaves.

62.

WHITE	BLACK
1. P—KB3	N—KB3
2. P—K4	N x P
3. Q—K2	N—N6
4. Q x P ch	Q x Q ch
5. K—B2	N x R mate

The diagram shows the mate.

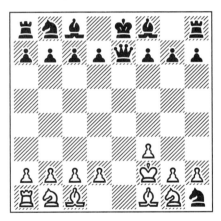

53. N, being the last letter in the word "seven." The sequence is the last letters of the words one, two, three, etc.

51. Alan is from New Zealand, Rita is from Britain, Eric is from America, and Don is from Indonesia.

134. 367 × 52 = 19,084.

125. Starting with the lowest of the three empty circles and reading clockwise, enter the letters "e," "n," and "t" so that "entitlement" can be spelled out.

131. The top left square of the 5 × 5 grid is 19, and the top left square of the 3 × 3 grid is 24.

10	49	48	47	8	9	4
11	**19**	37	36	18	15	39
12	20	**24**	29	22	30	38
7	17	23	**25**	27	33	43
44	34	28	21	**26**	16	6
45	35	13	14	32	**31**	5
46	1	2	3	42	41	**40**

74. Apart from using the information given directly, clues can be combined for extra information. For example, clues one and three can be combined to deduce that Angela is not from Staten Island. Working through, the result below then follows.

MANAGER	ACCOUNT	DISTRICT	CHILDREN
Angela	Aviation	Bronx	4
Brian	Marine	Staten Island	3
Chloe	Liability	New Jersey	5
Dick	Fire	Queens	1
Enid	Automotive	Brooklyn	0
Fred	Property	Manhattan	2

64.

A 4	a 2	b 9	B 4	c 1	Cd 2	0	D 9	e 9	f 2
Eg 7	5	F 2	h 9	G 5	6	4	Hi 7	7	4
I 8	8	j 1	J 9	1	K 1	k 1	0	5	l 1
3	m 1	L 4	0	n 3	Mo 9	0	N 2	p 9	4
Oq 1	2	6	P 2	9	1	Q 9	r 3	R 8	4
S 3	3	0	T 3	9	U 2	1	V 6	4	4

61. The answers to the clues are shown below. In each case, the first word is the one that is to be entered into the diagram:

¹M	²S	³S		⁴D	⁵S	⁶L
⁷P A L E S T			⁸S E C U R E			
N	D	A		T	I	A
⁹B I Z A R R ¹⁰E			¹¹A L T E R			
L	T	N		I	C	N
¹²C A ¹³T E R		¹⁴R E L I A N T				
	E		A		S	
¹⁵D I E T I ¹⁶N G			¹⁷S ¹⁸P E ¹⁹A K			
I	N	M	E	O		B
²⁰S C A L P		²¹D ²²E P O S I T				
U	G	A	D	D		D
²³S H E A R S		²⁴A S L E E P				
E	R	T	M	E		S

ACROSS
7. palest/petals
8. secure/rescue
9. bizarre/brazier
11. alter/later

12. cater/trace
14. reliant/latrine
15. dieting/ignited
17. speak/peaks

20. scalp/claps
21. deposit/topside
23. shears/rashes
24. asleep/elapse

DOWN
1. manila/animal
2. sedate/seated
3. star/arts
4. detail/dilate
5. suitcase/sauciest

6. learnt/rental
10. enraged/angered
13. teenager/generate
15. disuse/issued

16. impart/armpit
18. poodle/looped
19. abides/biased
22. edam/mead

59. The first school had 495 pupils, of whom 286 were boys; the two schools combined had 1,495 pupils, of whom 415 were boys.

71. The first drop should be from floor 14, and the maximum number of drops can be limited to no more than 14.

Suppose the first drop is from floor n. If the crystal breaks, then there is no alternative to dropping the second crystal from floor 1, then floor 2, and so on, up to floor (n – 1) at most. This would ensure that no more than n drops would be required.

Now suppose the crystal does not break on its drop from floor n. The second drop is then from floor (2n – 1), and if the crystal breaks here we start dropping the second crystal from floor n + 1, up to floor (2n – 2) at most. Again this ensures no more than n drops in total.

If the first crystal does not break, we continue advancing up the building by one less floor each time; i.e., by (n – 2), then (n – 3), and so on till we get to the top. We therefore need to find the smallest value of n such that n + (n –1) + (n – 2) + ... + 1 ≥ 105. (Remember, we already know that a crystal dropped from the 106th floor will shatter.)

The sum on the left-hand side simply gives the triangular number $T_n = n(n + 1)/2$, and if $T_n \geq 105$, we then have $n(n + 1) \geq 210$. The smallest value of n to satisfy this equation is 14.

107. D = 100. Each letter equals the number in whose name it first appears. Thus tWo, foUr, fiVe and so on. D first occurs in one hunDreD.

75. Let the train be t minutes early. The wife (driving at 36 mph) saved 5 minutes each way, so the man walked for t – 5 minutes. Because this saved 5 minutes' driving, he walked at 5/(t – 5) of her speed. If she had driven at 46 mph, she would have saved 4 minutes each way, so similar reasoning leads to the following equation:

$$\frac{5}{t - 5} \times 36 = \frac{4}{t - 4} \times 46$$

whence t = 50 minutes.

86. A = Orlando; B = Cincinnati; C = New Orleans; D = Washington, DC. The theme is American cities.

76.

Aa 7	0	Bb 3	c 1	5
C 8	d 2	1	D 9	e 9
E 4	5	Ff 8	6	4
G 3	2	0	H 7	6

52. **THIS** = 5,693, **THAT** = 5,625, **IT** is 95, and **THIS** × **THAT** × **IT** = 3,042,196,875.

72. $119 = \Sigma\Sigma\Sigma\Sigma\Sigma\sqrt{4} \ / \ \Sigma\Sigma\Sigma\Sigma\sqrt{4} + \Sigma\sqrt{4} = 26{,}796 \ / \ 231 + 3$
$268 = \Sigma(4!) - \sqrt{}\ \sqrt{4}^{\Sigma 4} = 300 - 32$
$336 = \Sigma\Sigma\sqrt{4} \times \Sigma\Sigma 4 + \Sigma\Sigma\sqrt{4} = 6 \times 55 + 6$

All integers from 1 to 336 can be made with three fours and the symbols given.

99.

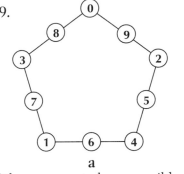 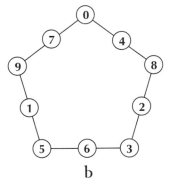

a   b

Other answers to b are possible.

26. The paragraph is unusual because, unlike this answer, it does not contain the letter "e."

8. Replace each letter in a country's name by the position of the letter in the alphabet. For example, Italy becomes 9 20 1 12 25. Goals scored is then the smallest difference between any pair of numbers, so Italy scores 12 − 9 = 3 goals.

The result of the final tie was therefore: Poland 1 Portugal 1.

106.

81. Label Samos Farm as shown below:

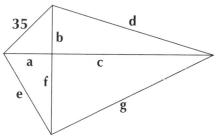

Thus $a^2 + b^2 = 35^2$, $b^2 + c^2 = d^2$, $c^2 + f^2 = g^2$ and $a^2 + f^2 = e^2$, where a, b, c, d, e, f and g are all different, integral and not equal to 35.

The unique integral solution to $a^2 + b^2 = 35^2$ is $21^2 + 28^2 = 35^2$. Other integral Pythagorean triangles with a side of 21 or 28 are:

$$21^2 + 20^2 = 29^2 \qquad 28^2 + 45^2 = 53^2$$
$$21^2 + 72^2 = 75^2 \qquad 28^2 + 96^2 = 100^2$$
$$21^2 + 220^2 = 221^2 \qquad 28^2 + 195^2 = 197^2$$

Assuming a is 21 and b is 28 (it does not matter which way round), f is 20, 72, or 220, and c is 45, 96, or 195. Knowing that $\sqrt{(f^2 + c^2)}$ is integral, the only possible values of f and c are 72 and 96. The area of the farm can now be calculated and is: $\frac{1}{2}$ (21 × 28 + 21 × 72 + 96 × 28 + 96 × 72) / 10 = (21 + 96) × (28 + 72) / 20 = 585 acres.

80. The way for Lynsey to win is to play the dashed line shown below. Any other move would allow Heather the opportunity to win.

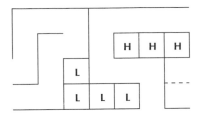

After claiming the two boxes in the bottom right-hand corner, Heather's best move is to open up the nine boxes at the top right and center and hope that Lynsey will take them. Lynsey would be wrong to do so, however, for she can win by the strategy shown below of taking just seven boxes:

		L	L	L	L
		L	H	H	H
	L	L	L		H
	L	L	L		H

Lynsey's sacrifice of two boxes forces Heather to open up the group of ten boxes on the left-hand side for Lynsey. The final result would be as shown below, with Lynsey winning by 21 boxes to 7.

L	L	L	L	L	L	L
L	L	L	L	H	H	H
L	L	L	L	L	H	H
L	L	L	L	L	H	H

Note that if Lynsey had originally offered Heather the chance of completing the two boxes in the bottom right-hand corner with a vertical line instead of the one shown, Heather could have taken control of the game simply by adding another vertical line to the bottom right-hand corner.

84. 95,759.

89.

Aa 1	b 2	7	c 3	d 3	6	e 3	f 2
B 1	0	g 2	4	C 3	h 5	6	8
7	D 2	4	8	8	3	2	0
E 6	5	6	1	F 1	1	2	7
G 9	i 8	0	j 1	Hk 8	4	l 6	4
2	I 1	1	7	6	4	9	8
J 6	9	6	2	K 4	1	4	1
L 1	1	3	8	9	8	9	6

130. A = Connecticut; B = Illinois; C = Wyoming; D = Wisconsin. The theme is the U.S. States.

85.

The diagram shows the *ends* of the matches. There are six squares of unit size, and two squares measuring 2 x 2.

83. $3,015,986,724 = 54,918^2$ and $6,714,983,025 = 81,945^2$.

94. Ask A, "Does B tell the truth more often than C?" If the answer is yes, then ask C the next two questions and if the answer is no, ask B. This question is designed to ensure that the second and third questions will not be directed at the man who lies at random.

Question two is: "Do the other two always give the same answer?" As the truthful answer is always "No," this question determines whether the man being asked is the one that is always truthful or the one that always lies.

Question three is: "Of the other two, does A tell the truth more often?" The answer will enable you to determine the status of the other two men.

78. Q is 67,980, and 54,321 × 67,980 = 3,692,741,580.

70.

3	71	5	23
53	11	37	1
17	13	41	31
29	7	19	47

126. $0.56, $1.20, $1.25, $1.50, $1.70, $2.00, and $2.50.

88. White wins as follows:

WHITE   BLACK
1. R – QR3   P – N6
2. R – R1   P x R (Q ch)
3. Q x Q mate

91.

	●		●				
●					●		
				●		●	
●		●					
	●						●
					●	●	
		●		●			
			●		●		

108. The statements can be rewritten as follows:
   • Today is Thursday.
   • Today is Tuesday.
   • Today is Sunday.
   • Today is Sunday, Monday, Tuesday, Wednesday, Thursday, or Friday.
   • Today is Tuesday.
   • Today is Wednesday, Thursday, Friday, or Saturday.
   • Today is Monday.

The only day that is not mentioned more than once is Saturday, so today must be Saturday.

93.

¹3	²5	³8	⁴8	⁵9	⁶6
⁷5	3	7	6	0	1
⁸1	2	3	4	6	7
⁹7	9	6	1	5	3
9	7	¹⁰1	7	3	9

10-Across comprises the last four cells of 3-Down, 4-Down, 5-Down, and 6-Down. Each of these is the product of two three-digit primes and therefore ends with 1, 3, 7, or 9. In no answer is a digit repeated, so 10-Across is a four-digit number that is the product of two two-digit primes and contains each of the digits 1, 3, 7, and 9. The only answer for 10-Across that meets these criteria is $37 \times 47 = 1{,}739$. By similar reasoning, 6-Down is 61,739.

The digits of 8-Across are in ascending order, have no digit repeated, and the sixth digit is 7. Using this information and the answers to 6-Down and 10-Across, a computer search will uncover the unique solution.

113. From the information given in the question, we know that the radius of the outer circle (the one on which A and B lie) is 3 times the radius of the inner, concentric circle through C and D. Thus, the circumference of the outer circle is 3 times the circumference of the inner circle, and so the arcs AB and CD are equal in length.

Since arc CD is more curved than arc AB, its ends will be closer together. Thus, the lines AC and BD are not parallel—they will meet down and to the left of the diagram.

77. A = goldfinch; B = eagle; C = partridge; D = nightingale. The theme is birds.

115. Vivienne Westwood had 153 outfits exhibited. The "3" represents the number of letters appearing only once in her name (i.e., the "s," "t," and "d"); the "5" represents the number of letters appearing twice (the "v," "i," "n," "w," and "o"); and the "1" represents the number of letters appearing three times (the "e").

118. Suppose n clients were picked, with 10n names in the complete mailing list. The clients picked were numbers 1, 3, 6, 10, ... with the final one being number n(n + 1)/2. Since the final one was the last name in the index, it follows that 10n = n(n + 1)/2, whence 20 = n + 1. Thus, 19 clients were chosen out of a total mailing list of 190 clients.

95. Begin by noting that the cake's area cannot be less than (1 x 10) + (2 × 9) + (3 × 8) + (4 × 7) + (5 × 6) = 110 inches². By trial and error, the smallest cake that will meet the requirements will then be found to be 9 × 13 inches, which has an area of 117 inches². The cut cake is as shown:

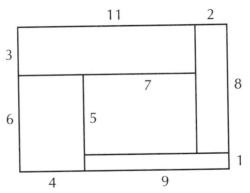

112. Barbara Easton weighs 117 pounds, after losing three pounds.
Anne Frost weighs 113 pounds, after losing two pounds.
Debbie Green weighs 101 pounds, after losing four pounds.
Carol Hope weighs 111 pounds, after gaining one pound.

124. 2 × $27 + 2 × $34 + $84 + $91 = $297 = 2 × $72 + 2 × $43 + $48 + $19. The answer is $27 + $34 = $61.

116. One solution is:

	3	5	
7	1	8	2
	4	6	

82. As with many puzzles such as this, the flaw is in the given diagram. A more accurate diagram is shown here:

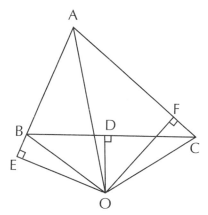

Proceeding as before:

AFO is congruent to AEO, so AE = AF and OE = OF.

BDO is congruent to CDO, so OB = OC.

OEB is congruent to OFC, so EB = FC.

Thus, AE + EB = AF + FC = AC ≠ AB, because AB = AE − EB.

105. A = Hyundai; B = BMW; C = Honda; D = Bentley. The theme is cars.

17. In addition to the information given directly in the question, note that if there is someone who last dined in restaurant A who will be dining next in restaurant B, then the person who last dined in restaurant B cannot be dining next in restaurant A. Working through the information given, the result below then follows:

NAME	CITY	LAST DINNER	NEXT DINNER
Ann	Auckland	Wholemeal Cafe	Farewell Spit Cafe
Ben	Dunedin	Collingwood Tavern	The Old School Cafe
Cathy	Christchurch	Milliways Restaurant	Wholemeal Cafe
David	Wellington	The Old School Cafe	Milliways Restaurant
Emma	Hamilton	Farewell Spit Cafe	Collingwood Tavern

117. The common total is 21. A = 3, B = 4, and C = 5.

96. A = mandolin; B = oboe; C = triangle; D = cymbals (symbols). The theme is musical instruments.

128. The sound of each letter in the top row is the same as a three-letter word that does not include the letter itself: sea, eye, eau (as in eau de Cologne), cue, and ewe.

40.
1. Egypt   5. Vietnam
2. Qatar   6. Senegal
3. Brazil   7. Algeria
4. Rwanda   8. Estonia

90.

C				
H	E			
E	A	R		
C	R	O	W	
K	N	E	E	L

111. The middle circle reads New Zealand, and the five six-letter words are "snooze," "secede," "casino," "meddle," and "Malawi."

129. You might have thought that the camp could have been in the vicinity of the South Pole at any point where a walk one mile east, after the mile south, took the explorer an exact number of times around the South Pole. This would mean that a walk one mile north would then retrace the walk one mile south and the explorer would then be back where she started. However, you would have been wrong, as polar bears do not live at the South Pole!

97. $1! + 4! + 5! = 145$.

38. Starting with the empty circle on the right and reading counterclockwise, enter the letters "u," "n," and "d" so that "underground" can be spelled out. The less common word "undergrounder" is also formed from this circle.

45. The equation **TIM × SOLE = AMOUNT** is sufficient, with a computer search, to solve this puzzle. However, the extra information provided enables the puzzle to be solved as follows:

Because **LEAST** and **MOST** both end in **ST,** and either **LEAST – MOST = ALL** or **MOST – LEAST = ALL,** then **L = 0.**

Substituting **L = 0** in **LEAST – MOST = ALL** and **MOST – LEAST = ALL,** then either **EA – MO = A** or **MO – EA = A.**

As **L = 0,** then **O ≠ 0** so **EA – MO ≠ A** and **MO – EA = A.** From this, **MO = EA + A, M = E + 1,** and **O** is even. As **L = 0, O = 2, 4, 6,** or **8** and **A = 6, 7, 8,** or **9.**

As **TIM × SOLE = AMOUNT,** then **M × E** is a number that ends with **T.** As we also know that **M = E + 1,** then **T = 2 or 6.** (Note that **T ≠ 0** because **L = 0.**)

If **T = 6,** then **S = 1** since **TIM × SOLE** is a six-digit number and **E = 2 or 7.**

If **T = 6** and **E = 2,** then **M = 3, S = 1** (see above), and **O = 4 or 8. O ≠ 8,** since **TIM × SOLE** is a six-digit number, and if **O = 4, A = 7** and there is no solution, so this combination is eliminated.

If **T = 6** and **E = 7,** then **M = 8.** However, then **A = 9** and **O = 8,** which is impossible because **M = 8.** This combination is therefore also eliminated, and **T = 2** because **T ≠ 6.**

Given that **T = 2,** then **E = 3, 6,** or **8** with corresponding values for **M** of **4, 7,** and **9.** Also, as **T = 2,** then **O ≠ 2,** so **O = 4, 6,** or **8** and **A = 7, 8,** or **9.**

If **E = 3** and **M = 4,** then **S = 1** as **TIM × SOLE** is a six-digit number. But **T = 2** and **S = 1** implies **A** is less than **6,** and **A = 7, 8,** or **9,** so this combination is eliminated.

If **E = 8** and **M = 9,** then **A = 7** and **O = 4.** As **TIM × SOLE** is a six-digit number, **S = 1 or 3,** but then there is no solution, so this combination is eliminated.

Therefore **L = 0, T = 2, E = 6, M = 7, O = 8, A = 9** and **S = 3,** from which **I = 5, U = 1,** and **N = 4,** giving **257 × 3,806 = 978,142.**

INDEX

Numbers refer to puzzle numbers.

The authors are always pleased to hear of new puzzles. If you have a puzzle you think we could use in our next book, please send it to us with details on its source and your suggested solution. If we use your puzzle, we will acknowledge your contribution. Our e-mail addresses are timsole@xtra.co.nz and marshalls@liz-and-rod-marshall.fsnet.co.uk.

What Is Mensa?

Mensa
The High IQ Society

Mensa is the international society for people with a high IQ. We have more than 100,000 members in over 40 countries worldwide.

Anyone with an IQ score in the top two percent of the population is eligible to become a member of Mensa—are you the "one in 50" we've been looking for?

Mensa membership offers an excellent range of benefits:
• Networking and social activities nationally and around the world;
• Special interest groups (hundreds of chances to pursue your hobbies and interests—from art to zoology!);
• Monthly International Journal, national magazines, and regional newsletters;
• Local meetings—from game challenges to food and drink;
• National and international weekend gatherings and conferences;
• Intellectually stimulating lectures and seminars;
• Access to the worldwide SIGHT network for travelers and hosts.

For contact information, see the next page.

For more information
about American Mensa:
www.us.mensa.org
American Mensa Ltd.
1229 Corporate Drive West
Arlington, TX 76006-6103

For more information about
British Mensa (UK and Ireland):
www.mensa.org.uk
Telephone: +44 (0) 1902 772771
E-mail: enquiries@mensa.org.uk
British Mensa Ltd.
St. John's House
St. John's Square
Wolverhampton WV2 4 AH
United Kingdom

For more information
about Mensa International:
www.mensa.org
Mensa International
15 The Ivories
6-8 Northampton Street
Islington, London N1 2HY